When the Grass Dances

VALERIE GILLIES and REBECCA MARR

Luath Press Limited

EDINBURGH

www.luath.co.uk

First published 2025

ISBN 978-1-80425-241-3

The authors' right to be identified as author of this book
under the Copyright, Designs and Patents Act 1988
has been asserted.

Printed and bound by
Robertson Printers, Forfar

Typeset in 11 point Sabon by
Main Point Books, Edinburgh

VALERIE GILLIES has composed poetry since the age of fourteen. A former Edinburgh Makar, poet laureate to the city, Royal Literary Fellow and an Associate of Harvard University, Valerie has been a literary arts practitioner in psychiatric and general hospitals with Artlink and a Writer in Residence in universities and libraries. She co-facilitated the creative writing workshops at Maggie's Centre, Edinburgh, for sixteen years, and has been a trainer with Lapidus Scotland. Her many collections include *Tweed Journey*, following the River Tweed from source to sea, and *The Spring Teller*, poems inspired by Scotland's wells and springs. Her work explores the healing potential of its environment, and this has an invigorating effect upon the reader.

REBECCA MARR was born in the Highlands and she has had a darkroom since childhood. She studied photography at Edinburgh Napier University. She moved to Orkney in 2007 for a Pier Arts Centre artist residency 'Art & Agriculture' working with farmers, and settled there. Rebecca works across digital and traditional darkroom techniques. Her subjects have included clouds, seaweed, Orkney's wild flowers and of course the grasses. She has contributed to over twenty publications, including several collaborations with archaeologist Mark Edmonds. She works with her husband Mark Jenkins on museum and community heritage projects.

Valerie & Rebecca first met in the mid-nineties, brought together by artist Kirsty Lorenz to run creative workshops with Artlink at The Royal Edinburgh psychiatric hospital. They have continued their friendship and support for each other over the years. *Men & Beasts*, a touring exhibition and publication in 2000, was their first collaboration. Two decades on, they embarked on a five year study of the wild grasses of Scotland.

Praise for *When the Grass Dances*

Informative as well as a joy to the senses.—ELEANOR MACLEOD, RANGER

This collaboration is utterly beautiful. The two are equal partners and symbiotic. Each is augmented by the other and converses with it.—JOHN GLENDAY, POET

A creative and healing embrace.—RISSA DE LA PAZ, FACILITATOR

Full of everyday riches.—KEN COCKBURN, POET AND TRANSLATOR

Books by the same authors

Valerie Gillies

Each Bright Eye: Selected Poems 1971–1976, Canongate, 1977
Bed of Stone, Canongate, 1984
Tweed Journey, Canongate, 1989
The Chanter's Tune, Canongate, 1990
The Ringing Rock, Scottish Cultural Press, 1995
Tweed Journey, Canongate, 1998
The Lightning Tree, Polygon, 2002
The Spring Teller, Luath Press, 2008
The Cream of the Well: New and Selected Poems, Luath Press, 2015

Valerie Gillies & Rebecca Marr

Men and Beasts, Luath Press, 2000

Rebecca Marr & Mark Edmonds

After Orcadia, Group 6 Press, 2022
Hand Held, Group 6 Press, 2024
Midhowe, Group 6 Press, 2025

In memoriam

Rebecca dedicates this book to her mother-in-law Betty.

*Valerie dedicates it to her grandparents in
Tigh-na-Monadh, their house on the moor.*

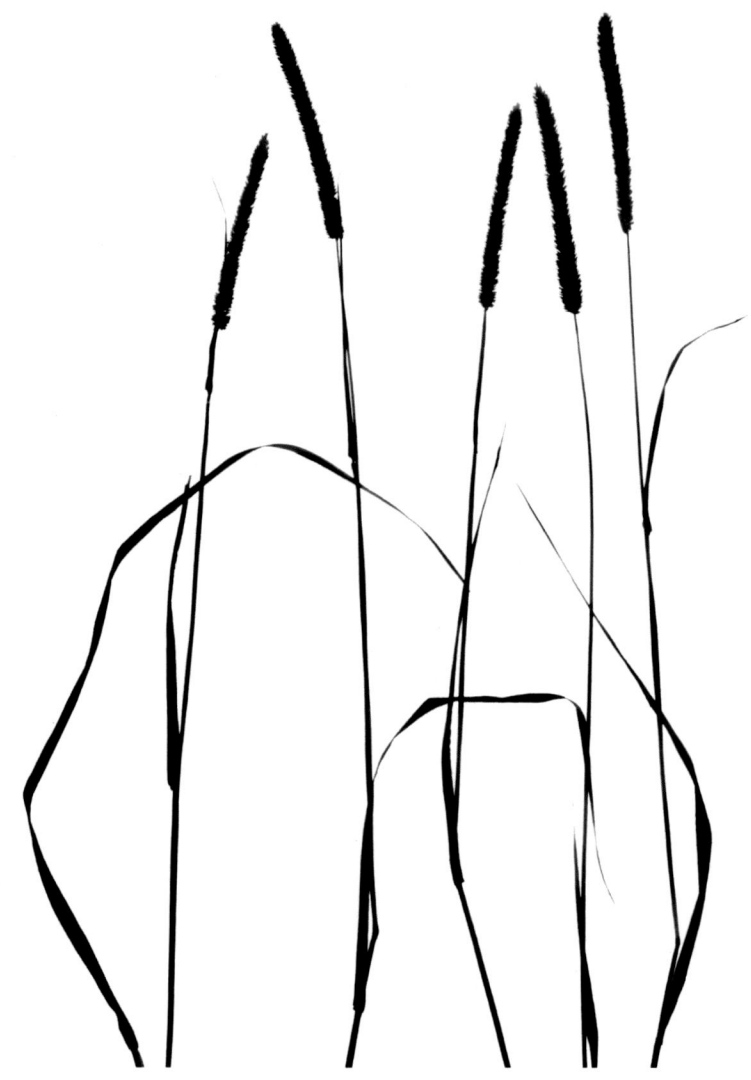

Timothy, *Phleum pratense*

Contents

Grass holds us together: an introduction

'We will accompany thee and lead thee through a grass-plot...'
John Gerard *Historie of plants, 1597.*

IT IS SPRINGTIME again and we are going to leave the road, setting foot among the grasses. A deep memory stirs, of Neolithic ancestors wandering with their grazing animals across open grassland and through forest glades. The grasses have grown alongside our species. The history of the grasses is integral to the world of human beings. The greensward has always reinvigorated humans and renewed their resilience in challenging times. Each footstep of ours resonates with the life of the wild grasses, they lighten our tread and revive us. Every spring is a time of discovery when we can enter the whirling dance of the living grasses through their growing season.

Early forms of grass appeared at the same time as the last dinosaurs. The arrival of grass allowed human beings to form nomadic tribal communities, accompanying their animals to summer pastures. For grasses to regenerate they need to be used. Once it was wild bison who grazed and trampled, encouraging the growth of grasses. Then the treading-in of grass seeds by the domestic animals of the first Bronze Age settlers sustained the enrichment of the grasslands.

Humans and grasses continue to have a close relationship. We rely on the grasses to nourish us bodily, whether we eat rice, grain or wheat or the animals that feed on the grasses themselves. Grasses thrive all over our world from the hottest to the coldest places, the wettest to the driest. Grasses have been overlooked in our society's state of plant blindness. They cover around a third of our planet; omnipresent but unnoticed. As the agrostologist Agnes Chase tells us, 'Grass is what holds the earth together.'

In another springtime, that of May 1867, the Victorian botanist

Margaret Plues hoped:

> to secure the attention of a large proportion of the observant
> for the elegant grasses now beginning their varied succession in
> our rich meadows and pastures. Once begun, we have no doubt of
> the acquaintance being succeeded by admiration, and ripening into
> friendship, nor of the cordial satisfaction resulting from the new
> study. We earnestly entreat our readers to throw themselves without
> delay into the pursuit of grass-lore and to begin to collect and to
> study at once, so that the present season may be fully utilised...

Acquaintance, admiration, friendship. We were entering into a
relationship with the grasses. Our fascination began to encompass
all the graminoids, beguiled by the beauties in our aye-close-by
guide, *The Observer's Book of British Grasses, Sedges and Rushes*.
Away we went with our notebooks, each in our own corner of
Scotland, and with our field guides, lenses, and plenty of Scots
sayings.

Every step of a walk, city or island, lowland or highland,
increased our knowledge and understanding. By focussing on a
particular aspect of nature, we were becoming attuned to our
subject to such an extent that everything about it held fascination.
We were compelled to look beyond the idea of grass being a
single entity. When we paid attention, we found that what we had
regarded as simply grass revealed itself as a complex and fascinating
family of plants. Looking along the road-verge or the shoreline, we
began to recognise that the grasses are distinct from one another. We
were starting to see the grasses. It felt revelatory. As botanists Tom
Cope and Alan Gray remind us in *Grasses of the British Isles*:

> The grasses are an extraordinarily successful group and their
> success has been based on three recurring themes: (1) their ability
> to adapt to the changing environment; (2) their ability to coexist
> with man and his grazing animals; and (3) their possession

of a very distinct life-form that remains faithful to a single architectural idea but which has almost endless, and often very ingenious, variations.

We were open to natural wisdom and we started to think about what the grasses could teach us. Grass can survive being trodden down and crushed, it can withstand grazing, it grows from the root not the tip. These characteristics are useful to reflect on while we search for resilience ourselves. Through re-growth and regeneration, grass makes a comeback. 'Live, horse, and ye'll get gress': the frozen winter waves of grass will be soft and verdant come spring. Grass symbolises life in all its growth and freshness. It invites us to reinvigorate ourselves, it enlivens us. Walking across a patch of grass becomes sustaining, a sense experience that has an impact on the body.

We respond to the greensward. Green spaces are good for us. Green is comforting and refreshing: the spring grass brings warmth, the summer grass is filled with life. Always the colour of hope, green is the sign of annual renewal, of awakening life. The twelfth-century mystic and Benedictine abbess Hildegard of Bingen used the term *viriditas* (greenness) by which she meant the greening power of the creator. Hildegard used it to describe the earth's greening and fecundity, but also the soul's greening, '*opus Verbi viriditas*': the work of the Word is greenness.

In his book *The Forgiveness of Nature: The Story of Grass,* agricultural journalist Graham Harvey praises grasslands as the purifiers of the earth's atmosphere, remarking that 'grasslands store as much carbon in the organic matter of their soil as temperate forests and far more than tropical rainforests.'

He insists that:

Every acre of park, every patch of green space between city buildings, every sunlit meadow is contributing to the survival of the planet, taking in carbon from the atmosphere and locking some of it safely in the soil.

Once we view the grasslands in this light, he can promise that we will receive 'the eternal gift of grass, the freedom of the open sky, the freedom to be fully alive'.

Scotland has wonderful grasses. Scots, the auld leid, was Valerie's childhood language, shared with her grandparents in a rural environment, a language native to the grasslands. She has drawn on her own living memories, recalling a life among moorland and pasture: finding a lapwing's nest on the moor; putting a hand into the outline of a hare's form to discover if the lair is still warm; learning to cut grass with a sickle, or swinging a scythe along with her grandfather; filling a hay-net for a horse or moving kye to fresh pasture.

Rebecca, living in Orkney, knows the wind in the grass blows through time. Watching sheep graze on top of the green mound of Maeshowe, the Neolithic tomb, she sees how those first farmers share the space with us. The shy Orkney voles, who arrived 5,000 years ago with those first farmers, make their runs in the grass. The woven holes they leave tell you they are there. Salt wind whips the sea grasses as below ground the marram knits a net to hold the beach. From the air the whole of Orkney can appear green.

When the wind is blowing through grass on the moor or on the shoreline, the ground appears to move and shimmer and there is a great green presence about it. Looking at grass and listening to words about the grasses has made us more joyful and more connected to nature. A green door opens. We hope this collection does the same for you.

In preparation for meeting the grasses, here is a brief glossary:

Anther	The pollen-bearing, commonly yellowish or purplish part of the stamen
Floret	One of the small flowers that together make up a spikelet
Inflorescence	An arrangement of flowers on the floral axis; a flower cluster

Ligule	Small projection from the top of the leaf sheath; it may be membranous or a rim of hairs or rarely, missing entirely
Node	The joint on a stem from which a leaf can arise
Panicle	A branched inflorescence with spikelets borne on stalks
Rhizome	An underground stem, whitish
Spike	An unbranched inflorescence with spikelets attached directly to the stem
Spikelet	The basic unit of a grass inflorescence, comprising one or more florets
Stamen	The male organ of the flower, comprising a filament with anther at the tip
Stigma	The terminal branch or branches of the female organ of the flower, where pollen lands
Stolon	A creeping stem growing on the soil surface and rooting at the nodes

Adapted from Agnes Chase's *First Book of Grasses*, co-written with botanist John Crossley

Previous page: Harray Loch, Orkney, July

PART I

The Characteristics of Grass

IDENTIFICATION OF GRASSES and sedges can be tricky but is also very rewarding. Year on year as our confidence in naming them grew, we found ourselves speaking their names out loud: 'Ah there you are, Timothy; we meet again Wavy Hair-grass; it's you, Star Sedge'.

In our poems and photographs we have encompassed the graminoid sedges and rushes, alongside the true grasses. Graminoid refers to the grass-like appearance of these plant families, with their thin blade-like leaves and minute flowers, though they differ in many other respects. We found this diagnostic rhyme helpful:

Sedges have edges, rushes are round,
Grasses are hollow, what have you found?

– generally true but not quite foolproof.

On first making acquaintance with grasses, we found them complex and difficult to understand in all their variety. Soon enough though, we came to discern them by those essential parts that make grass grass. The underlying architecture is constant and quite simple, the variation in detail almost infinite.

One guide has been Agnes Chase's classic *First Book of Grasses: Structure of Grasses Explained for Beginners*, first published in 1922. Lesson one is on morphology, the structure of grass and the names used to describe the various parts. The culm (aerial stem) is (mostly) hollow, with one to several solid nodes along its length. The leaf blades alternate in rows on opposite sides of the culm. They vary between species – for instance in being flat or in-rolled, hairy or smooth, with tips hooded or not. Each leaf is attached to a sheath that surrounds the culm and at this attachment you will find, if you peel back the blade, a thin membrane facing the stem called the ligule. This tiny part of grass requires a hand lens to reveal its shape – a useful clue to identify which grass you are encountering. Inflorescence is the name for the flowering part; it may take the form of a loose branching cluster, or a more or less dense cylinder. In flowering season the grasses can express themselves in brightly coloured anthers and delicate feathery stigma. With each species timing its shedding, the air swirls with pollen, viable only briefly and reliant on the wind to find a partner. There is a lot going on, and it's been going on all around us wherever we live.

While many grasses reproduce freely by seed dispersal and are often the first colonisers of bare ground, others can spread by creeping runners. Then the strong roots hold earth together; they can bind shifting sands and mitigate soil erosion. A vast area of grass can be just one plant.

Tufted Hair-grass, *Deschampsia cespitosa*
Brinkie's Brae, Stromness, Orkney, June

On Time

Now is the time for the flowers of the grasses
to be at their best.
In May and June, some say,
they have their own hours for opening.

Meadow-grass opens between 4 and 5am,
Quaking-grass and Tussock grass about an hour later,
Meadow Fescue and Cock's-foot between 6 and 7,
Foxtail, Cat's-tail and Sweet Vernal-grass between 7 and 8.
At 11 the Dog-grass opens.

Around noon, the Wood Melick, the purple Molinia,
the Mat-grass and the Sea Lyme-grass unroll.
About 2pm, the Brome-grass is nodding,
the Wild-oat about 3,
Dog's Wheat and Twitch grass at 4.

Wavy Hair-grass opens between 5 and 6,
while Fog grass opens twice, downy and pale,
at 6 in the morning and 7 in the evening.

All these grasses like to be on time,
each flower takes twenty minutes to open completely.

Found poem, from *The Observer's Book of British Grasses, Sedges & Rushes*

Brinkie's Brae, Stromness, Orkney, August

grass in the round of life
brings colour and light

Quaking-grass

Briza media

Shakie tremlies
Siller shakers
Shivering grass

Waverand at ilka wind
and thirled by a fitstep
on approche

Gang warily
by the quaking-grass
that grows aroon the bobbinqua

Dried Quaking-grass, *Briza media*

Water Whorl-grass, *Catabrosa aquatica*, Sandside, Deerness, Orkney, July

Water Whorl-grass

Catabrosa aquatica

Water whorl-grass of the running streams

Sweet Vernal-grass, *Anthoxanthum odoratum*, Brinkie's Brae, Stromnes, Orkney, May

Sweet Vernal-grass

Anthoxanthum odoratum

The hill-pasture is a pleasant place
when sweet vernal-grass is blowing,
its flavour always good to taste
while the summer hayfield's growing,
filled with essential oil of coumarin, flushed,
and its scent strongest when cut or crushed.

Bog Hair-grass

Deschampsia setacea

They're found in bogs
and peaty pools:
dense tufts,
their leaves hair-like,

purple and pale yellow
spikelets,
the bent awn brown
and twisted.

They have no value
as pasture:
plants becoming rare
as the wild blue hare.

Detail of a specimen of *Deschampsia setacea* from the Royal Botanic Garden Edinburgh
(RBGE) (Ù00861991_6)

Craa's Nest below Clicknafea, Rackwick, Hoy, Orkney

See the patch on the heather muir?
Thon's the Covenanter's Grave,
And it's as green as green can be
Whaur he was said tae faa.

The story which inspired the poem was given to the poet and her aunt by a shepherd living in the South Lanarkshire cottage where an earlier shepherd had offered shelter to a wounded Covenanter boy after the battle of Rullion Green. The Covenanter fled uphill to the moors to save the shepherd's family from persecution by his pursuers. He died on the crest of the hill, looking towards his homeland in Galloway. No heather is ever seen on the spot, only the greenest of grass grows there.

A similar account is told in Orkney. On Clicknafea in Rackwick, Hoy, there is a green patch called Dead Boy's Grave. The site appears on a map that pre-dates the Covenanters' landing in Rackwick. It is believed to be the site of the unmarked grave of a boy chased as he abandoned a disease-ridden ship

youth of the grass,
tooth of the grass

Marram grass, *Ammophilia arenaria*, NO.4 Barrier beach, Burray, Orkney, May

Mat-grass

Nardus stricta

Mat-grass found uprooted on the heath,
too harsh to eat, avoided by the sheep,
take these tufts into your hand,
feel the grass of bairnheid land.

Where wiry stems of mat-grass grow,
bright purple spikelets in two rows
are always pointing just one way,
a finger-hold upon a summer day.

bairnheid – childhood

Mat-grass, *Nardus stricta*, Brinkie's Brae, Stromness, Orkney, May

Field Wood-rush

Luzula campestris

Sweep's brushes grow on high heathland,
throwing off shoots from tufted rootstock.
A stem sheathed in dark-green leaves
startles by its signal. Look again
at the yellow diamond of the anthers
set in these smuts of near-black flowers.

They are taking April for their own,
thriving through a month of frosts
to grow into a grass that can be called
by its old country name of *God's Grace*.

Field Wood-rush, *Luzula campestris*, North Hill, Papa Westray, Orkney, May

Tufted Hair-grass, *Deschampsia cespitosa*

Windle Strae

Deschampsia cespitosa

In June, you will want to walk again
where the old map shows a farm by the name
of Windle Strae, those long thin stalks
and coarse leaves of tufted hair-grass.

On a corner of the hospital building-site
it meets you, standing tall to greet you
with a wave of proliferating spikelets.
It is growing on the spoil-heap,

preparing to outlast the new construction.
It surprises you with silvery panicles,
this is how you will always find it
on the slope where its name is standing.

Wild-oat

Avena fatua

Wild-oat is random, a weed of arable crops
That may or may not be in any field.
It is very obvious, standing high above the barley.
Any farmer would be glad for you to take
As much as possible, and some will always escape.

Found poem from botanist John Crossley

Dried Wild-oat *Avena fatua*

Viviparous Sheep's-fescue, *Festuca vivipara*, Brinkies Brae, Stromness, Orkney, June

On Brinkie's Brae

Festuca vivipara

Fescue grass shoots up
in leafy tufts
with spikiness
to match a bantam-cockerel's crest

As wise as a field o gress

Happy Valley, Stenness, Orkney, May

Previous page: Cock's-foot, *Dactylis glomerata*, Brinkie's Brae, Stromness, Orkney, June

PART 2

The Movement of Grass

IT IS THE late Cretaceous period here on earth. Grasses, relative latecomers in the plant world, have established themselves. They leave us a message, a grass spikelet trapped in amber, a memo from a hundred million years ago to say, 'we are here'. Around the edges of the forests some grasses start to appear. Land bridges allow this worldwide family to travel freely. The earth is very different at this time, before division and drift split up the continents.

Much later now, the earth has shifted to a more recognisable map, it's the time of the woolly mammoth and it roams the grasslands, its mammoth feet trampling seeds into the soil.

Closer to our own time, ten thousand years ago, humans begin to utilise the association of grasses and animals. This is the Holocene, the epoch we inhabit now.

Closer still, the Neolithic herders are clearing trees and creating pastures for their beasts. The grasses reward them and an accord between *poacea* and people is sealed. Pastoralism has arrived.

Grasses enjoy freedom: freedom to roam, carried on the wind or by animals, and freedom to settle, easily establishing themselves. These characteristics have made them a success and now they occupy the earth, surviving in the extremes: coldest, hottest, wettest and driest. They are survivors and have evolved to coexist with humans and animals. C.E. Hubbard tells us in his book *Grasses* that we don't always realise that

these associations of grasses are almost entirely artificial in origin and due to the continuous labours of many generations of ancestors, together with the cumulative action of the grazing and treading of their domestic animals. Under our climatic conditions and on most soils, these artificial grasslands, when removed from the control of man and beast and left to the effects of competition and natural selection, gradually revert to scrub, and in most cases from scrub to forest.

Humans harnessed the grass, rooting it to fields and taming the wild grass seed to become cereals. The message in amber from a hundred million years ago is echoed in the amber-coloured fields of grain as they move with the wind.

Star sedge, *Carex echinata*, near the Ring of Brodgar, Orkney, July

Star Sedge

Carex echinata

I am the tiny star sedge
looking to the sky above my head

I'm growing, spreading star-wise
closely linked to starry skies

Wavy Hair-grass, *Deschampsia flexuosa*, Harray Loch, Orkney, July

Wavy Hair-grass

Deschampsia flexuosa

Light and airy flowerheads
On branches thin as sewing thread;
July brings wavy hair-girss
To cover all the moorland:
A swathe of pink, of purplish mist
Swayed by every tirl of wind,
Good grazing for a heft of sheep,

With some to carry home asleep
In your arms, as light as air,
Your bairn with tousie swirls of hair.

Barren Brome

Bromus sterilis

you turned up with me
growing by my bench
in early summer
tall and handsome
broad leaves tapering
to a fine point
slender stem with clusters
of drooping spikelets
swaying on the breeze
a weed of the wayside
with loose nodding panicle
flowering beside me

Barren Brome, *Bromus sterilis*

Reeds, *Phragmites australis*, Lochan Sgeireach, Assynt, December

Reeds

Phragmites australis

Reeds we bring from the tide
spring from a new root
they wave by a child's side
      move with a human foot

Common Sedge, *Carex nigra*

Dancing Grasses

Tap foot on drumbeat,
the ground reacting equally
to each step, pressing through the foot,
rocking the dancer,
knee and foot are stalk and shoot
as he dances, as he dances.
Two young men from the Omaha nation
begin a warrior dance, wearing
white yarn fringes, grass ribbons
around their ankles, they go low
to the ground then rise up again.
Sweetgrass and blades of beargrass
hung on dancers' bodies:
green grows the leaf
tied with a grass that never breaks,
to honour their ancestors and this space.
The grass shows them the way to be
dancers who bring good energy
to the pow-wow ground for others.
Here with Lakota friends, the pipe-carrier
says to me, 'Now it's the Inter-tribal:
it is time, you are going to dance.'
Going round with all the others
the ground feels alive
where the tribes have danced all day,
dancing grasses, dancing grasses.

Great Wood-rush

Luzula sylvatica

Yes by a burn in Achnagairn woods
the gleam that lives among the leaves
silvers our land, lights luminous globes,
lamps that shine in the darkest weather.

Great Wood-rush, *Luzula sylvatica*, Achnagairn, Kirkhill, Inverness-shire, May

False Oat-grass

Arrhenatherum elatius

Admired by all grass-lovers
in full flower takes over road verges
rapid-growing deep-rooted
swiftest among grasses
sprints across waste ground
takes over slopes and screes
its panicles glisten in the sun
with metallic lustre green and lilac
long thin stems round and shining
most suitable for hay.

False Oat-grass, *Arrhenatherum elatius*

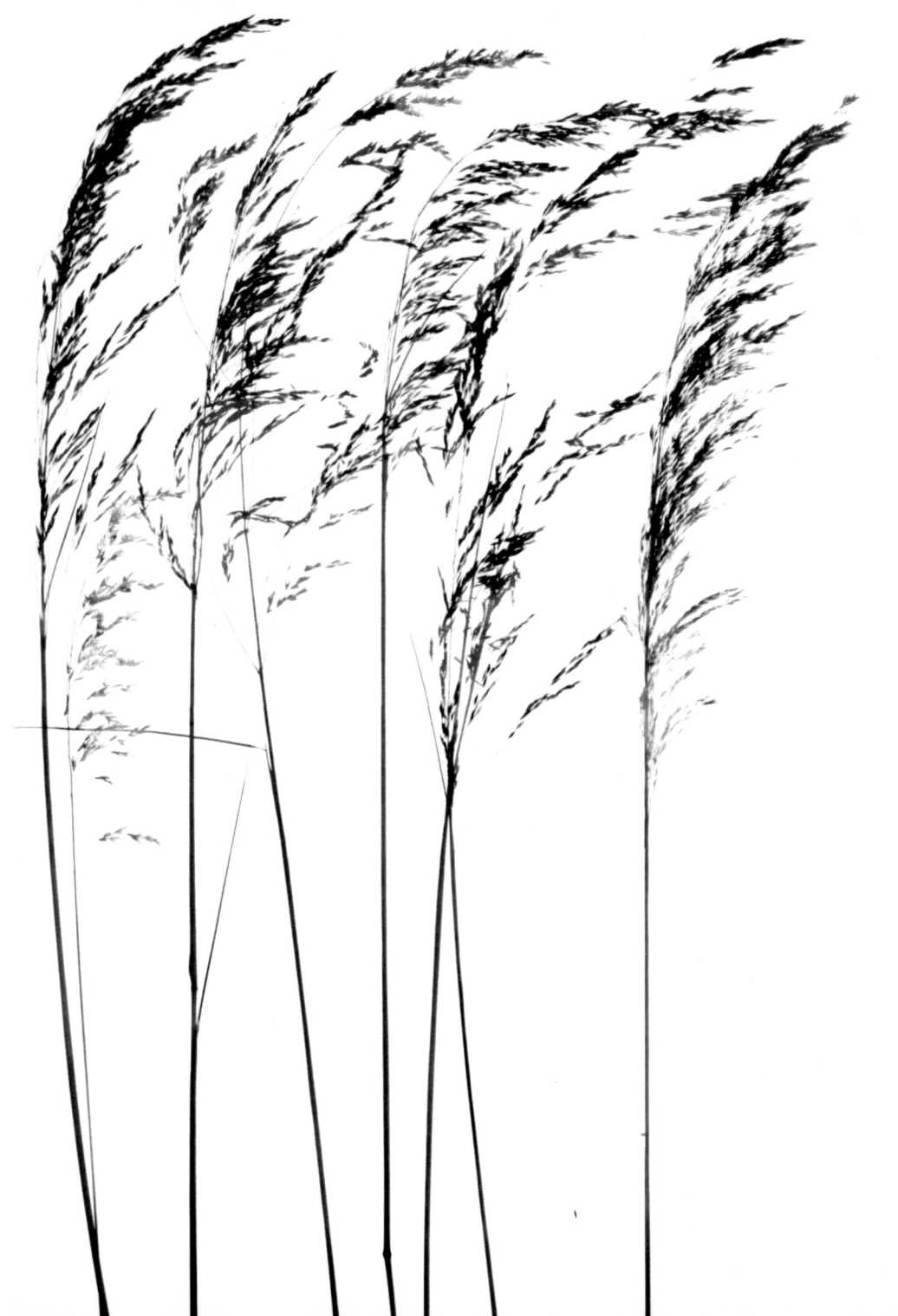

Tufted Hair-grass

Deschampsia cespitosa

Familiar grass, its panicles silver-grey, showy,
quivering in the breeze, flashing light-rays
from glossy glumes, airy and glittering, rising
out of hassocks, rough caps, growing in any soil,
can even tolerate spoil heaps near heavy metals.

Tufted Hair-grass, *Deschampsia cespitosa*

Silver Hair-grass, *Aira caryophyllea*

Silver Hair-grass

Aira caryophyllea

Beyond the sandy path
a slope opens to the sky.
A gleam and a glint
dazzle, burnished silver
stands out in a birr.

Strange, the phenomenon of light
flashing from the grass.
Glossy panicles shake loose
and stems are blown
into brilliance by the wind.

Around the head of the land
silvery changing-grass
shines its halo. These things exist
through rays. Ready to move on,
the grasses walk alongside.

Bale of Hemp

Cannabis sativa

A whole bale of hemp
washes ashore at Grass Point
on Mull — so fitting

Detail of a specimen of *Cannabis sativa* from the Royal Botanic Garden Edinburgh (RBGE) (Ù00405499_6)

By Hundland, Papa Westray, June

Floating Sweet-grass

Glyceria fluitans

Floating by streamside
in slow-moving fresh water –
pale Ophelia:

cows wade far into the pool
to crop these slender leaves.

Previous page: Reedmace, *Typha Latifolia*, known as Cat's-tail, Eileanreach, Inverness-shire, June

PART 3

Creatures of the Grass

LUCKY IS THE lass who grows up among rolling hills and moors in wild hare country. Looking all around her for other forms of life, she knows that she too is being observed. As she stops by an old peat hag, on a path hollowed among the heather, an eye is regarding her. A hare is lying in its form, the lair on top of the ground that it has shaped to rest and nestle in. It is unsure whether to run or stay, but after a minute it seems to recognise the girl. It is clear that there could be several pairs of eyes watching, alert, on what seems to be an empty slope.

If the slope is in the lee of the wind, this is a place where hares will be lying, just as they have always done. The child will come to recognise several individuals over the years, and they will know who she is, too. Half a century can pass and new generations of wild brown hares will keep running by. When the field below the hill is freshly ploughed, it looks like heavy going, but a hare can move lightly across the surface, spreading its toes to keep moving, in the same way that it does over snow.

Encounters with hares are never forgotten. The weather, the surroundings, the exact place where they were lying, ears back, ready to run. Then there is the moment they lift off like a bird, soaring across the hillside, jinking and turning uphill where their long hind legs give them the advantage over any predator.

See them feed, choosing a single spikelet or green stem out of a tuft of grass. Making this choice reveals their favourites among the plants.

Spring is the season to see three hares rather than one. The March hares are boxing, in their mating ritual when the jill rejects one or more of her jacks.

Among the unforgettable moments are the ones when the hare's brown coat seems to glow. If the hare emerges from a background of darker woodland and it is lit by the sun, then a natural alchemy changes it into gold:

> a golden hare rests in the birchwood,
> touched thousands and thousands
> of times by the sun.*

In spring the grasses start to hum with activity; animals and birds are making use of the grasses for food and shelter. One creature uses grasses for both, the cuttack. It wasn't until the late 19th century that the Orkney Vole was recognised as distinct from other species. John Gullie Millais (son of the Pre-Raphaelite painter whose Ophelia floats beside pond sedge), was fishing on the Loch of Stenness and began to wonder if the voles weren't altogether different.

The Orkney Vole is unique to the archipelago; in fact this subspecies is the only vole in Orkney, and they've been here since the Neolithic. The settlement of Skara Brae was revealed one day in 1850 when a storm tore the grass off the dunes, and there it was, a complex of dwellings. In these stone walls were tucked the bones of Orkney Voles. No-one yet knows how the bones came to be there, or in the other Neolithic sites where they have been found, or even how the voles arrived in Orkney in the first place.

Plump on grasses, sedges and rushes, mother cuttack can produce almost fifty pups a year. But the population is imperilled by loss of habitat, and if she goes then the birds of prey that rely on her also go: Cattieface, Katabelly and the Moosie hawk. Grasslands with waves of older grasses create a thicket that provides the raw materials for vernacular vole architecture, tunnels of grass with crafted circular entrances. A home of grass in which to shelter from predators and raise young, the circle of life in a circle of grass.

* From 'The Rink', *The Cream of the Well*.

Cattieface   Short-eared Owl
Katabelly   Hen Harrier
Moosie hawk   Kestrel

Adapted from Tim Dean's *The Orkney Pocket Book of the Orkney Vole* 'the cuttack – an unsung hero'

Meadow Foxtail, *Alopecurus pratenis*, Brinkie's Brae, Stromness, Orkney, June

A Bestiary

Rat's-tail, Cat's-tail,
Mouse-tail, Fox-tail,
Bristlegrass

Hare's-tail, Dogstooth,
Rabbitfoot, Cockspur,
Feathergrass

Frog Rush, Toad Rush,
Goose-corn, Canary-grass,
Ticklegrass

Flea Sedge, Nit-grass,
Deergrass, Squirreltail,
Adder's Tongue

Bird's-foot, Hart's-tongue,
Horsetail, Stag's-horn,
Sheep's Fescue

Cow Quakes, Crab Grass,
Totter Grass, Beetle-grass,
Twitch!

Marsh Horsetail

Equisetum palustre

Horsetail shows up in the peat,
it's what the dinosaurs ate
before there were any grasses.
All the horsetails are
poisonous to horses.

Marsh Horsetail, *Equisetum palustre*, Harray Loch, Orkney, June

Hare sequence

Lepus europaeus

He's so well hidden,
you might walk over the hare,
if it weren't for

the glisk of one eye
as he sinks into his form

Grass is growing up
the middle of the old road.
The doe hare pauses:

her two leverets suckle
while she rests from her running

Hare's-tail Cottongrass, *Eriophorum vaginatum*

Drumbeg, Assynt, December

At this early hour
you will be able to smell
the scent of the hare

The hare flies uphill
where his long back legs will give
him the advantage

Orkney Vole

Microtus arvalis orcadensis

Orkney Vole hole

Brinkie's Brae, Stromness, Orkney, June

Pygmy shrew

Sorex minutus

pygmy shrew
rushy roo

Purple Moor-grass, *Molinia caerulea*, the Old Rackwick Road, Hoy, Orkney, May

Cock's-foot grass, *Dactylis glomerata*, Brinkie's Brae, Stromness, Orkney, June

Cock's-foot grass

Dactylis glomerata

A lintie o a lass rins uphill
tae the pasture field.
On the hip o the brae
the auld grey horse is lyin doon.

A worn-oot yaud
on his watch knowe,
his ee is far awa wi it,
lookin tae the heathery hills.

He's waitin on the bairn
tae coorie in by his shouther.
She'll pu a tait o grass for him,
the cock's-foot he likes fine.

Thegither in companionrie,
the bairn beginnin
tae look ower the nest,
the grey horse beginnin

tae look aboot him
for a last *circumspice*,
they forgaither on the brae,
wide-warld waukin.

lintie, a sprightly lass; *yaud*, an old horse; *tait*, tuft; *coorie*, cuddle; *shouther*,
shoulder; *thegither*, together; *companionrie*, companionship; *circumspice*,
look about you; *forgaither*, keep company; *wide-warld waukin*, wide-awake

Above Yelda reservoir, Stromness, Orkney, June

Glenhead Shepherd

Through the winter, the yowe aye remains
within a mile o the hoose,
but when the gude weather sets in
an the draw-moss shows abune the grun,
she's aff tae whaur ye see her noo —
sax mile richt oot-owre the mountains.

draw-moss: Bog cotton

Fleckie

Fleckie the red-and-white spotted cow
licks up grass from the hill-pasture.
Her lip mulls over fresh young leaves,
tall yellow buttercups are her garland.

Below Yelda reservoir, Stromness, Orkney, June

Heather and Purple Moor-grass, *Molinia caerulea*, Rackwick, Hoy, Orkney, May

The Writing Lark

Emberiza citrinella

A flock of yellowhammers are in the hedgerow.
Ae yellae yite undulates in flight

To its nest of moss, in a tuft of coarse grass.
Three eggs, a purplish clutch; fine lines blotched

And inked with brown are boldly jotted down.
The scribbling lark has made these marks,

A cryptic watchword inscribed by the bird
Whose message begs, *Dinna tak ma eggs!*

Swan Colours

Cygnus olor

Swan flying solo
belly and underwings blue
over the water

standing on grass the cob swan's
breast takes on a greenish hue

Vacated swan's nest, Loch of Stenness, Orkney, July

Netherton Road, Stromness, Orkney, June

Cattieface

Asio flammeus

This year there have been plenty of voles.
Early in June, walking across the open moors,
I see a hawk-owl perched on a single old fencepost.
She takes off and flies directly at me.
Hey, owl of the day,
You short-eared owl. She flies so close to me,
I think a falconer has lost his bird.
Does she want to land on my arm?
She slices past then flies at me again.
This time she locks onto my eyes with hers,
Gives me the death stare in yellow.
She carves the air alongside me, steers around
And comes back to dive at the whippet
In the long grass, who lowers her eyes.
What have we done to her? Somewhere
On this wide moor must be her nest,
Sheltered by surrounding grass and reeds.
She must have two-three chicks hidden.
Dull white round eggs, or pluffed-up fledglings,
I don't have time to look for them before
She swings round again, two more passes by my face
I won't forget, she could have my head off.
She lands on a turf dyke to watch our retreat,
Ruffles her feathers, hisses her scorn for us.
Sssssssss
Uh-uh-uh-uh-uh-uh
Chef-chef-chef

Glow-worm

Lampyris noctiluca

Starshine fills the valley, overflows
the brim. Close as a coloured globe,
a glow-worm on a stalk of grass
lights her cold lamp, takes
a shine to neon green.

Midnight, Eileanreach, Lentran, Inverness-shire, July

Eileanreach, Lentran, Inverness-shire, July

Grasshoppers bend knees
in the cathedral of stems:
they look up to leap

Meadow Brown

Maniola jurtina

On sunny days she's always on the wing
dusky brown   autumn brown
she delights in open ground

She's agile over hedge and scrub
cocoa brown   mocha brown
she delights in open ground

how fast she flies in upland meadows
brindle brown   bracken brown
she delights in open ground

She skims the moorland and the downs
fuscous brown   fawn brown
she delights in open ground

Brinkie's Brae, Stromness, Orkney, June

Yorkshire-fog, *Holcus lanatus*, Eileanreach, Lentran, Inverness-shire, July

Scotch Argus

Erebia aethiops

We promised we would bring her here
to this grassy flank of the south-facing hill
where it enjoys the first warming rays of the sun.
High above her old house, the stable and fields,

it's hard to climb the hill over rough ground
where purple moor-grass grows in lush tussocks.
We disturb scores of Scotch Argus butterflies:
they go bobbing around us, flickering browns

who haunt this hillside as the slope takes wing.
They have been a chrysalis first, then a caterpillar
feeding on blades of grass; they become butterflies
in dark brown velvet, the black ones freshly hatched.

Rows of false eyes with white pupils on their wings
help them survive a bird or lizard on the hunt.
We are here for the scattering of Jean's ashes
when light radiates around us in the rushes,

dusky butterflies in a sunburst, who are rising
in airy lightness, free to become a blessing.
One dewdrop from their wings cures every pain.
'Do you see all the butterflies? This is paradise.'

Live, horse, an ye'll get gress

Perennial ryegrass, *Lolium perenne*

Previous page: Midsummer's night, Brinkie's Brae, Stromness, Orkney

PART 4

Working with the Grasses

A HANDFUL OF grass pulled from the field has many uses and in this chapter we embrace the utility of grass. Take simmans, for example, a two ply rope made of grass, straw, rushes or heather.

Making simmans

Take a length of bundled grass, fold it in the middle to make a loop. Work each side from the top of the loop twisting and turning towards you to plait the lengths. Add in more folded grass as needed. Tuck it up under the twist to give more lengths of grass to work with. The sneud (twist) is done by one hand while the other keeps the rope taut. As the rope grows, pass it over your shoulder, around your waist and under your arm using your body to keep tension on the growing rope.

The rope is stretched out along the ground to take out any lirks or snarls before being wound up into a clew. A person lying on the grass ball and being able to touch the ground on either side with their fingertips measures a clew.

The double twist in the simmans prevents it from unravelling and it can be cut in lengths.

This grass rope is useful, vital even, for many purposes on the croft:

Securing the stack: to create a net to hold haystacks tight against the wind.

Comfort for a horse: to make a flackie, a saddle of simmans to protect a horse from a burden. Or a wazzie, a horse collar made of twisted grass rope and covered in sacking. Horses used to nibble grass escaping from other horses' wazzies.

Thatching a roof: layers of parallel lines of simmans are overlaid with layers of loose straw finished off with a layer of simmans weighed down by flagstones. Well built, the roof will last two winters.

Winter warmth: strae-beuts made from lengths of simmans wound under a boot and twisted up the leg. The friction created by the rope when walking sends a warm glow through the body. It is recorded that one winter forty men were chastised by a minister in the parish of Sandwick for wearing strae-beuts to the kirk.

Simmans underfoot and overhead.

Adapted from *Simmans, sookans and straw backed chairs* by Janette Park, Honorary Curator of Stromness Museum.

Bog cotton, *Eriophorum angustifolium*, Harray Loch, Okrney, June

Bed-socks

Eriophorum angustifolium

You can spin soft yarn
from bog cotton, knit bed-socks
for your wedding-night

Vasculum, 'little vessel', a small case made of tin that botanists took out to the field for carrying freshly collected specimens. This one in the herbarium is cylinder-shaped, with a long lid opening on one side. It holds 36 different types of grasses tied with name-tags showing habitats and soil types, and 60 glass bottles containing examples of seeds. A sales kit for the seeds supplier.

Sutton's vasculum, circa 1900, Royal Botanic Garden Edinburgh

Sutton's Vasculum

Grasses and Seeds
(Herbarium, Royal Botanic Garden Edinburgh)

Crested Dog's-tail
for all best pastures, sheep pastures, lawns and pleasure grounds

Wood Meadow-grass
for pastures, lawns or parks overshadowed by trees

Rough Cock's-foot
for moist places under trees, valuable for 3 or 4 years' ley

Wild-oat
a mischievous weed in corn crops

Soft-brome
inferior grass, usurping place of better sorts

Marsh Foxtail
Alopecurus geniculatus... USELESS

'I shouldered my tin vasculum, and went ashore.'
J Ball, *Notes of a Naturalist in South America*, 1887

Timothy

Phleum pratense

Now Timothy, already fair,
shoots up among the meadow-grass,
appears all over fields
where summer sun will bleach
the hay and fodder plants to white.

Timothy, *Phleum pratense*, Twingness, North Ronaldsay, Orkney, June

Soft rush, *Juncus effusus*, Waulkmill, Orkney, March

Using Soft Rush

Juncus effusus

Rush bends to every touch
bright green smooth stems
children plait to make bracelets

Pliant, woven into bee-skeps
or twisted into simmans cord
a rush-rope to fetch a pony

The saddle-bags made from floss
the rushes strewn on the floor
made into mats or chair-seats

It's August for harvesting rushes
pulled rather than cut
for the basket-maker

Rush bows to every change
we're peeling the stems for
the one white continuous pith

to make into rush-wick lights
held in a rush-nip holder
burning with a soft flame

Green grow the rashes O!

Westray, Orkney, September

132

Brigid's Cross

A white cow follows the saint
through a miraculous field of grass.
Brigid calms the storm,
makes butter for the poor,
takes reeds and weaves a cross
to tell what happened.

On St Brigid's Eve
over Eire and Alba
her influence heals
in many places:
in Traquair, Dunsyre, Melbost Borve,
springs flow among the reed-beds.

Craa's foot of Crested Dog's-tail grass, *Cynosurus cristatus*

While cows are grazing
you've all the time in the world
to weave a craa's foot

craa – crow

Crested Dog's-tail grass, *Cynosurus cristatus*, Stromness, Orkney, June

136

Crested Dog's-tail grass

Cynosurus cristatus

Crested Dog's-tail grass
grows wiry strong stems to plait
straw for summer hats

Straw Angus

Angus sits cross-legged in the grounds
tying leaves loosely, working them snugly.
Every day he's making ropes and clothes
out of grass, twigs, wool and hay.

Strong hands reject weak stalks,
cable-stitch netting sunlight.
The knitter takes up the jacket
the jacket alone enters the forest.

Hospital clothes smell of hot salt, bleach.
Straw Angus' clothes are made to last,
his moccasins, his leaf slippers,
his grass boots will step onto the shore.

He has a new purpose for rope.
Against the day of the big storm
he has a halter for a pony in hand
leading him home to the island.

For Angus MacPhee 1915–1996.
At the outbreak of the Second World War, he joined the Lovat Scouts with his
father's horse (the horse was later bought by an officer for £50). He was sent for
training in the Faroes. In 1941 he became ill and remained in a psychiatric hospital
in Inverness for the next fifty years, weaving among the woods and wards of Craig
Dunain. In 1996 he returned home to his family in South Uist, where he died.

Craig Dunain Hospital grounds, Inverness, August

A tussock taken to school
for a stool

Near Castle of Burrian, Westray, Orkney, April

On May morning

tak ae drap o dew fund on fresh girss

Behind Stromness Kirk, First of May

A green turf is a guid mither

North Hoose, Rackwick, Hoy, Orkney, May

Looking over to Hoy from Citadel, Stromness, Orkney, September

On Drowsy Brae

'Whit are ye daein here, on Drowsy Brae?
Letting the gress grow aneath ye, in amang
this saft brome, weel-kenned as sleepies?'

Forwandert, we're doverin ower,
takkin a rip o pluff-gress for a pillow
whaur it is nid-nod-nodding.

Oor darg maks us sair forfochten
and taigled wi aa the chainges,
we've lain doon, tyke-tired.

We'll streek oor length on Drowsy Brae
for that'll keep oor banes green.
We'll sleep as soond as a peerie.

We'll mind o this, when we wauken,
oor fowk were aye made o gress,
bairns o the yird an o the universe.

forwandert, weary with wandering; *doverin ower*, falling asleep; *pluff-gress*,
Yorkshire fog; *darg*, work; *sair forfochten*, exhausted; *taigled*, tired, harassed;
tyke-tired, dog-tired; *yird*, earth;

*Drowsy Brae is where a Bronze Age beaker was found, at Shieldhill in
Lanarkshire.*

Previous page: Marram, *Ammophila arenaria*, No. 4 Barrier beach, Burray, Orkney, June

PART 5

Sounds of the Grass

GRASS MURMURS WITH words at the edge of our remembering, the sound of names that the grass can still recall.

The voice of the moorland and the wide pasture belongs to the whaup, the curlew, who wheeples with its rising cry and gives rippling notes in the descent. This flight song has been described as far-carrying, or melancholy, or even bubbling, but there is one word which is more accurate, and that is 'longing': the call to return to the moors, the open slopes and the sky.

There are other sounds in the air, too. The deep hoots and quick wing-flaps of the short-eared owl flying by day greet us from a field near Kirkwall airport. It lands on an old fence-post to watch where we are going, its yellow eyes fierce to behold in its cattieface.

In the dusk a different creature is throbbing with a drumming sound, eerie because it is neither song nor call, but the air vibrating through a snipe's outer tail-feathers as it makes a short steep dive above the marsh. Called the moss-bleater or heather-bleater from this bleating sound, and the nyuckfit from its cry when ascending, the snippo is a bird of the bogs and damp meadows.

As a bairn Valerie only knew the lapwing as the teuchat, or the peewit, as in 'a flichter o peewits'. This is a good word with which to observe a flock of lapwings in their wallopie flight with rounded frying-pan wing-tips. In Orkney their name is teeo or teeick.

Another moor-bird is the laverock or skylark, who soars to a great height, up to 150m, almost invisible to the eye. Detected by the ear, it sings in this song-flight, climbing higher till it reaches 'laverock-heich', as high as the laverock soars, where it stays to sing for a while, with a waterfall of whistling notes. The skylark is a ground-living bird who nests in a tuft of grass, a buss o gress, only becoming a sublime singer when it flies up into the sky.

Down at grass level you can hear the sounds of the smaller winged creatures. A chorus of grasshoppers sing a whirling, clicking song, a grass-opera. The high pitched hoverfly comes in, then the rapid buzzing of the honey bee and the heavy buzz of the bumble. The butterflies and moths are almost silent but for the faint noise of their soft wings beating through the air.

With an ear to the ground you can pick up the vibrations of the Orkney Vole, the cuttack or volo, making its way through its grassy tunnel. The field mice, those timorous beasties, rustle. The moppie's hind paw drums out a warning whud, a carrying sound to alarm the other rabbits on the grassy slope.

Back on the muirs of Valerie's bairnhood, there is the low sound of scales sliding on dry grasses. An adder 'from her sunning-spot among the rocks speaks her hissy whihe sound with her big yellow mouth.'*

* Taken from 'The Green Well of Scotland', *The Spring Teller*, Valerie Gillies, Luath Press

Hushle

Hushle
the way wind crosses a field
sounding like grass waves
passing through widening circles
hushle

the lightest skiff becomes a skirl
the gentlest sowff becomes a swoof
as a shake-wind blows in gusts
hushle

grass is growing from the ground
moving everything within it
life coursing through every being
hushle

hushle, a strong wind; *sowff*, murmur, puff; *swoof*, swishing sound;
shake-wind, blustery wind

Old Finstown Road, Orkney, June

Verracott, North Ronaldsay, Orkney, June

Ah kin hear the gress growin

Ribbon Grass

Phalaris arundinacea var. *picta*

Ribbon grass
rustles in the breeze

long leaf blades
striped green and cream

phalaros bright
brilliant seeds

painted grass
gardener's garters

fly your
parti-coloured streamers

Reed Canary-grass, *Phalaris arundinacea* var. *picta*, Faravel, Stromness, Orkney, June

The Wind-Birds

Numenius arquata

While life lasts, look up
if you hear her far-carrying cry.
Over blue moor-grass
come the songs on the wing,

the heartbeat *kvi – kvi – kvi*
whistles across high uplands,
the slow gliding *courlee – courlee*
above her nest on tussocky ground.

Here her greeny-buff eggs
mottled and tashed with brown
hide the beginning of song
packed under smudged crowns.

Moorland, haunt of the whaups
who are kin to the wind,
between earth and sky they skirl
the *wheeple – whauple* of it all.

tashed, blotched; *whaup*, curlew

Rackwick, Hoy, Orkney, May

Peewit

Vanellus vanellus

On tap o the muir, walking hameward,
'Mind whaur ye're gaun,' says granfaither.
Ah luik doon at ma buits, haltit alangside
a scart in the yird, lined wi beusty gress
and heather sprigs. A clutch o fower dusky eggs
are laid in a circle, pointy ends inward.

'When we were laddies, if we were oot
aa day on the hill, we wad licht
a wee fire tae cook an eat thaim.
We wadna dae it noo, the peesies
are no sae mony as they yased tae be.'

Wallopie wings are flochtering abune us,
whaur a tappit green and purpie burd skirls:
pwae – widdle-weep, i – weep, i – weep,
cheee – o – weep, peesweep

peewit, lapwing; *scart*, shallow scrape; *beusty*, of last year's grass;
wallopie, flapping; *flochtering*, flickering; *tappit*, crested

Warebeth, Orkney, December

Hundland, Papa Westray, Orkney, June

164

How to Call in a Field of Long Grass

For a cat,
Cheetie-pussy, chatty-puss!

For a dog,
Iskay, iskay!

For a rabbit,
Mappie, map-map!

For a hen,
Chookay, tuck-tuck!

For a pig,
Gussie, gus-gus, grumfay!

For a calf,
Sucky, souk-souk,
troo, troo, troo!

For a cow,
Hurlie, hurlie-hawkie,
pree-leddy, proochie, chay!

For a horse,
Coap, coap, jee-up, how!
Woa.
Stawn.
Baak, Baak.

Calling the Cattle Home

in homage to Charles Kingsley (1819–1875)

'O Mary, go and call the cattle home,
And call the cattle home,
And call the cattle home,
Across the sands of Dee.'
The western wind was wild and dank with foam,
And all alone went she.

Aye, kye, kye, kye
Troo troo troosh

Pwroo, prooaa, pwray laidee
Pree may, pruitchee leddy
Pree-cawfay, pree-cawfay

Hurly, hurly hawkie
Chay

Crom-crommie, crommie
Kye, kye, kye
Halloa, moylie

But still the boatmen hear her call the cattle home
Across the sands of Dee.

Holland, Papa Westray, Orkney, June

Yorkshire-fog

Holcus lanatus

fussy punds
pluff-grass

Yorkshire-fog, *Holcus lanatus*, Polytunnel, South Hamar, Westray, July

Pendulous Sedge

Carex pendula

The wind gaes reeshlin through risp gress
till a wheesht comes at the stillin o the air:
quaiet gies a sough, mair a glisk nor a soond.

risp gress, sedges; *wheesht*, silence, hush; *sough*, whisper, murmur; *glisk*, perception

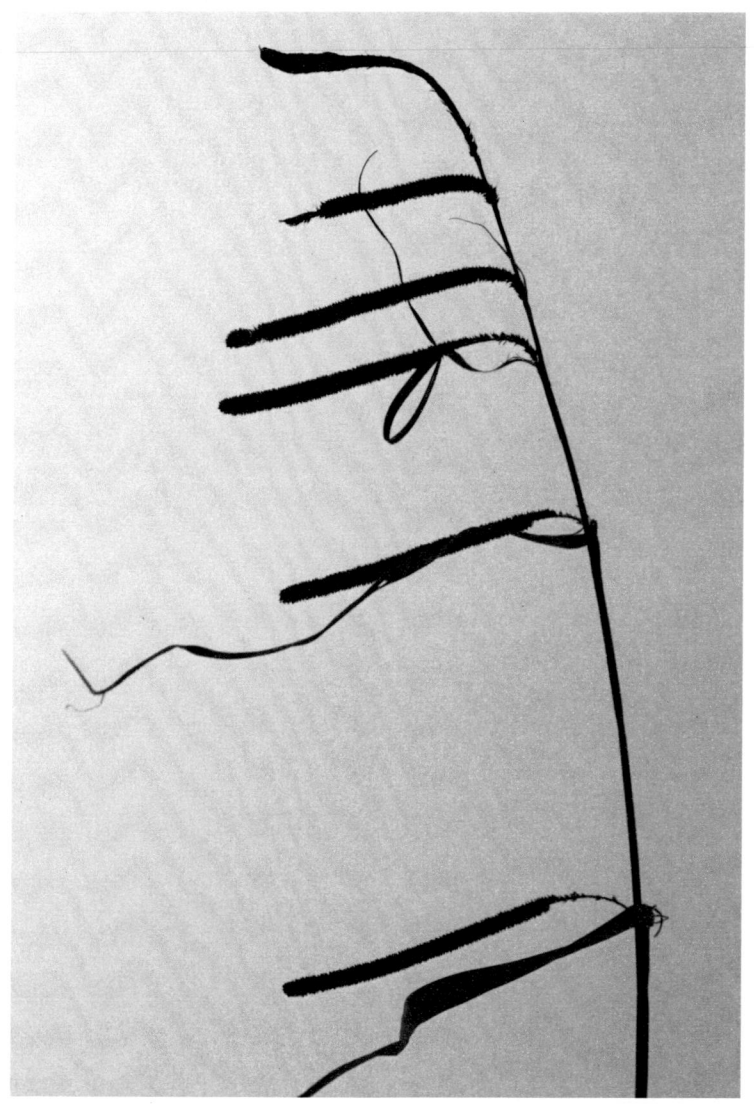

Pendulous Sedge, *Carex pendula*, Stromness, Orkney, June

Whistle

This is the moment you know why
your grandfather showed you
how to slit a blade of grass
and whistle through the space

Harray Loch, Orkney, June

Previous page: Brinkie's Brae, Stromness, Orkney, May

PART 6

Renewal of the Grass

GRASS ABOVE THE ground sustains humans bodily, feeding the world whether by direct consumption or via the animals who themselves eat grass. As Chapman writes in *An Introduction to the Grasses*:

> ...in a hungry world grasses are the centrepiece of agriculture and when we look at one damaged environment after another, grasses offer us some of the best hopes for rehabilitation.

Grasses can also sustain the human soul, giving us the greenness we need to soothe our minds and reconnect us to nature wherever we are. Grass grows between the cracks in pavements, along the roadside, in our gardens, parks and meadows, it is accessible. It also has the potential to sustain our future, our continued existence.

Species-rich grasslands are valuable carbon stores, locking away carbon in roots and soil. Living soil, aerated by earthworms, is nutrient rich, fed by the grassroots. That depth of storage makes it a stable carbon sink. Trees store the majority of their carbon above ground, grasslands store theirs mostly below. The deep down storage protects it from wildfire and disease and subsequent carbon release. We need woodlands and peatlands and we need grasslands.

Graham Harvey in *The Forgiveness of Nature: The Story of Grass* writes:

> Soil is not an inert material. Its mineral particles are enmeshed in a teeming mass of lifeforms whose myriad activities provide the starting point for life on earth. Humus is the hub of a whirling, rhythmic dance, an explosion of living energy which regulates the health of the planet. And chemical farming is steadily destroying it.

When we started this book it was as a response to the revelation we felt when we realised grass was not just one thing but a multitude of species. Moreover we realised that multitude of species was responsible for the sustenance of many other species. Grass offers hope. It grows from the root not the tip, it survives extremes and it is one of the first plants to germinate in waste ground. Restoration of grasslands and renewal of our esteem for them could guide us onto the path of good health.

Grass roots

grows from the root not the tip

Marram

Ammophila arenaria

Marram, the grass which binds
the young sand dunes
its strong roots
sometimes twenty feet long
creep through shifting sand

its sea-green leaves
slowing down the wind
a glossy grass
protects the coastline
constructs the ecosystem

planted for this purpose
it creates vast areas
as the dunes become fixed
and as other plants colonise
marram gives way to them

Marram, *Ammophila arenaria,* No.4 Barrier beach, Burray, Orkney, June

Warebeth, Orkney, December

Ilka tummock, sometimes bricht, sometimes derk.

All winter long

All winter long, like a dog,
the grass rolls over and plays dead.

Now the wind whistles,
the sun beckons,
'Up! Up with the spring!'

Suas leis an Earrach!

Near Skara Brae, Orkney, December

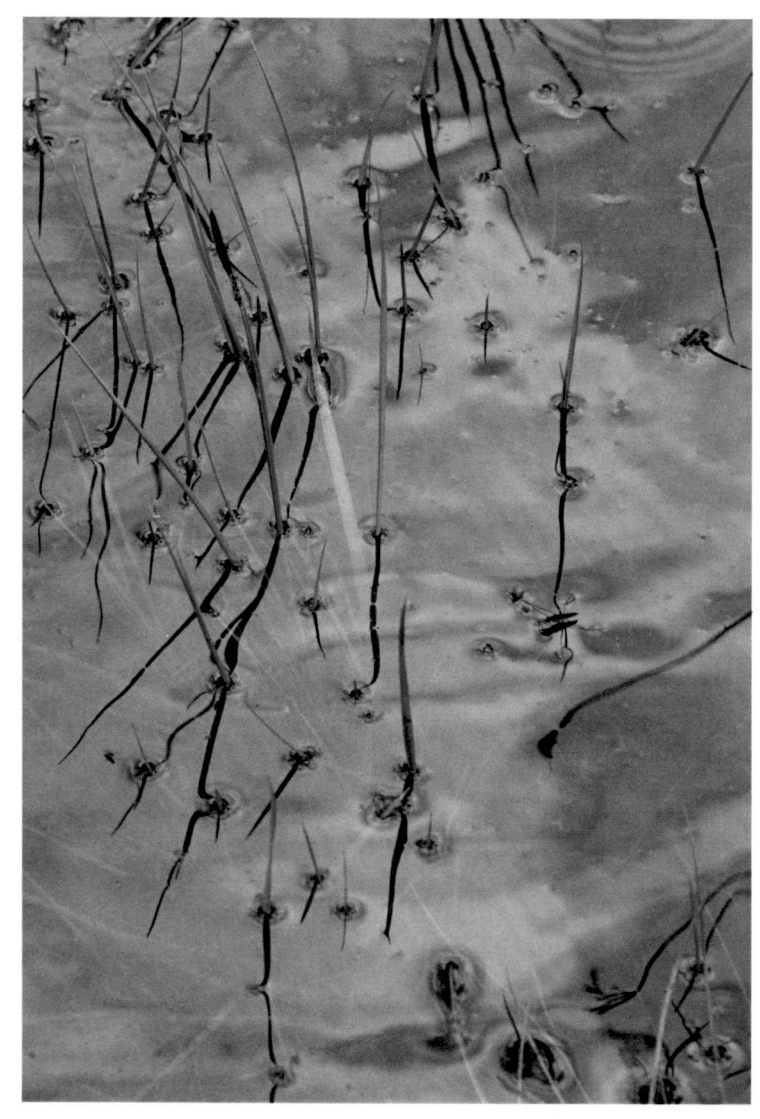

Sawmill, Newtonhill, Lentran, Inverness-shire, June

Bright green of the grasses around the spring
show the place where you'll find healing

healing is always possible

Verracott, North Ronaldsay, Orkney, June

Common Reed, *Phragmites australis*, Loch Bad an Og, Culkein Peat Road, Drumbeg, Sutherland, December

River Island

from Dante's *Purgatorio*, Canto 1, lines 100–105

Questa isoletta intorno ad imo ad imo,
*   là giú colà dove la batte l'onda,*
*   porta dei giunchi sovra il molle limo:*
null'altra pianta che facesse fronda
*   o indurasse, vi quote aver vita,*
*   però che a le percosse non seconda.*

All around this little island in its reaches low
      down there where the wave is beating,
      tall reeds from soft mud can grow:
no other plant can live there, bearing
      leaves or hardening in its prime,
      that will not bend when tides are battering.

Virgil Washes the Stains of Hell from Dante's Face with Dew

from Canto 1 of Dante's *Purgatorio*

Ei comincio: 'Seguisci li miei passi...'

And he began to say, 'Keep close, my son,
      let's turn round now, for if we go on this way
      the level loses height and slopes down to low ground.'
The hour for matins had begun to flee
      before the dawn's advance, while from this distance off
      I recognised the shimmering of the sea.
We wandered along the lonely plain
      like someone who searches for the road he's lost
      and feels, until he finds it, his efforts are in vain.
When we'd arrived where the dew can resist
      the sun, and because it's always cool there,
      it evaporates slowly, its dampness persists,
my maestro outstretched his hands with gentle care
      spread open on the fresh grass of the place,
      while I, of his purpose well aware,
held up my tear-stained face to him, unbidden;
      he wiped and brought my true colour to light,
      that hue which Hell had hidden.

Point of Ness, Stromness, Orkney, May

Soft rush, *Juncus effusus*

196

Soft Rush

Juncus effusus

Rush is soople, shairp and thin,
Fine for gaun again the wind

Holy-grass in flower

Hierochloe odorata

A rare grass
lights up the field,
its sweet scent
is all around

the shimmer-grass
glows with the light
given off by
all living things

holy-grass has its own
spikelets, its own
spreading flowerheads
and its own holy shape

Holy-grass, *Hierochloe odorata*, Harray Loch, Orkney, May
Next page: leaves of Holy-grass, *Hierochloe odorata*

Holy-grass, a blessing

Hierochloe odorata

Holy-grass is sweetgrass
on chapel floors strewn wide,
sweetgrass is holy-grass
running streams fructified.

Braids of gold and green
their own scent will keep,
hung above beds serene
to bring a blessed sleep.

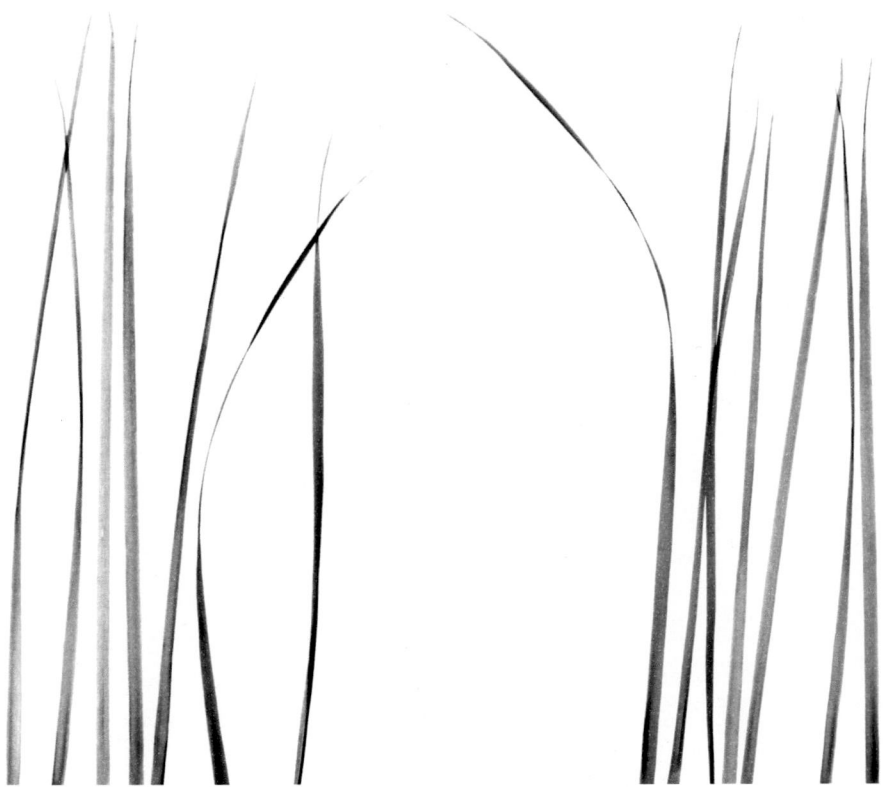

The gress is a warm freend

The Old Rackwick Road, Hoy, Orkney, May

Stour falls

Bide here while girse grows and watter rins

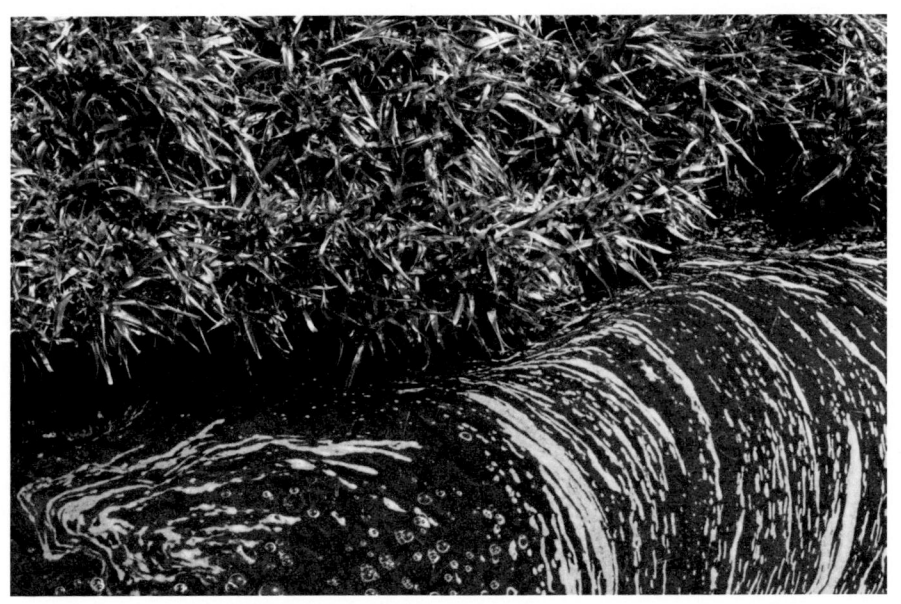

Stour Falls, Rackwick, Hoy, Orkney, May

List of Species

Barren Brome, *Bromus sterilis*
Bog cotton, *Eriophorum angustifolium*
Bog Hair-grass, *Deschampsia setacea*
Cock's-foot grass, *Dactylis glomerata*
Common sedge, *Carex nigra*
Crested Dog's-tail grass, *Cynosurus cristatus*
False Oat-grass, *Arrhenatherum elatius*
Field Wood-rush, *Luzula campestris*
Floating Sweet-grass, *Glyceria fluitans*
Great Wood-rush, *Luzula sylvatica*
Hare's-tail Cottongrass, *Eriophorum vaginatum*
Hemp, *Cannabis sativa*
Holy-grass, *Hierochloe odorata*
Marram grass, *Ammophila arenaria*
Marsh Horsetail, *Equisetum palustre*
Mat-grass, *Nardus stricta*
Meadow Foxtail, *Alopecurus pratensis*
Pendulous Sedge, *Carex pendula*
Perennial Rye-grass, *Lolium perenne*
Purple Moor-grass, *Molinia caerulea*
Quaking-grass, *Briza media*
Reeds, *Phragmites australis*
Ribbon Grass, *Phalaris arundinacea*
Silver Hair-grass, *Aira caryophyllea*
Soft rush, *Juncus effusus*
Star sedge, *Carex echinata*
Sweet Vernal-grass, *Anthoxanthum oderatum*
Timothy, *Phleum pratense*
Tufted Hair-grass, *Deschampsia cespitosa*
Viviparous Sheep's-fescue, *Festuca vivipara*
Water Whorl-grass, *Catabrosa aquatica*

Wavy Hair-grass, *Deschampsia flexuosa*
Wild-oat, *Avena fatua*
Yorkshire fog, *Holcus lanatus*

Acknowledgements

The artists are grateful for the support of their families and friends, in particular Liam and Mark.

The artists would like to give special thanks to:
John Crossley, Consultant Ecologist, Plant Recorder for Orkney.
David Harris, Herbarium Curator, Royal Botanic Garden Edinburgh 2001–23.
Lesley Scott, Assistant Herbarium Curator, Royal Botanic Garden Edinburgh.
Max Coleman, Science Communicator, Royal Botanic Garden Edinburgh.
Neil Leask, Custodian, Orkney Museums.
Janette Park, Curator, Stromness Museum.
Katy Firth, Exhibitions Assistant, Stromness Museum.
The late Jean Robb, microbiologist.
Mark Edmonds, archaeologist and author.
Tim Dean, naturalist.
Jennie Renton, book-woman
Maggie's Centre, Edinburgh, where a grass box of the poems and photographs is held.
Canongate Press and Luath Press where some of the poems first appeared.

Thank you to Gavin MacDougall and all the team at Luath Press.

The artists were supported by the National Lottery through Creative Scotland.

Further reading

Geoffrey P Chapman, WE Peat, *An Introduction to the Grasses (Including Bamboos and Cereals)*, CABI Publishing , 1992

Agnes Chase, updated by Lynn G Clark & Richard W Pohl, *Agnes Chase's First Book of Grasses: Structure of Grasses Explained for Beginners*, Smithsonian Institution, 1922, 1996

Thomas A Clark, *The Threadbare Coat*, Carcanet, 2020

Tom Cope & Alan Gray, *Grasses of the British Isles*, Botanical Society of the British Isles, 2009

Richard Fitter, Alastair Fitter & Ann Farrer, *Guide to the Grasses, Sedges, Rushes and Ferns of Britain and Northern Europe*, Collins, 1984

Graham Harvey, *The Forgiveness of Nature: The Story of Grass*, Jonathan Cape, 2001

CE Hubbard, *Grasses*, Penguin, 1954

Robin Wall Kimmerer, *Braiding Sweetgrass*, Milkweed, 2013

Joyce Laing, *Angus MacPhee Weaver of Grass*, Taigh Chearsabhagh Trust, 2000

William Milliken & Sam Bridgewater, *Flora Celtica*, Birlinn, 2006

Anne O'Dowd, *Straw, Hay & Rushes in Irish Folk Tradition*, Irish Academic Press, 2015

Janette Park, *Simmans, Sookans and Straw Backed Chairs*, Orkney Heritage, 2004

Roger Phillips, *Grasses, Ferns, Mosses and Lichens of the British Isles*, Ward Lock Ltd, 1980

Margaret Plues, L Reeve & Co., *British Grasses*, 1867

Frederick Warne & Co Ltd, *The Observer's Book of Grasses, Sedges & Rushes*, 1974

Lynda Weekes, Mark Wright, Una Fitzpatrick, *Identification Guide to Ireland's Grasses*, National Biodiversity Data Centre, 2016

Index of first lines

Luath Press Limited

committed to publishing well written books worth reading

LUATH PRESS takes its name from Robert Burns, whose little collie Luath (*Gael.*, swift or nimble) tripped up Jean Armour at a wedding and gave him the chance to speak to the woman who was to be his wife and the abiding love of his life. Burns called one of the 'Twa Dogs' Luath after Cuchullin's hunting dog in Ossian's *Fingal*. Luath Press was established in 1981 in the heart of Burns country, and is now based a few steps up the road from Burns' first lodgings on Edinburgh's Royal Mile. Luath offers you distinctive writing with a hint of unexpected pleasures.

Most bookshops in the UK, the US, Canada, Australia, New Zealand and parts of Europe, either carry our books in stock or can order them for you. To order direct from us, please send a £sterling cheque, postal order, international money order or your credit card details (number, address of cardholder and expiry date) to us at the address below. Please add post and packing as follows: UK – £1.00 per delivery address; overseas surface mail – £2.50 per delivery address; overseas airmail – £3.50 for the first book to each delivery address, plus £1.00 for each additional book by airmail to the same address. If your order is a gift, we will happily enclose your card or message at no extra charge.

Luath Press Limited
543/2 Castlehill
The Royal Mile
Edinburgh EH1 2ND
Scotland
Telephone: 0131 225 4326 (24 hours)
Email: sales@luath.co.uk
Website: www.luath.co.uk

The diversity of grasses is so important and is being remembered just as it's being lost. I loved this beautiful collaboration.
AMY LIPTROT, AUTHOR OF *THE OUTRUN*

The beautiful clarity of focus in this book will ground you, encouraging you to stop and listen to the grass growing. A verdant gathering intended to calm and restore. Spend time among the grasses and walk on with a heightened awareness of this overlooked yet vital plant family.

A celebration of greenery in its many wondrous forms and in every changeable season — from rushes to sedge, wild oats to hemp — and we find it shivering with life and beauty. This is florilegium as devotional text, a botanical catalogue of great artistic ambition.
CAL FLYN, AUTHOR OF *ISLANDS OF ABANDONMENT*

Luath Press Ltd.
543/2 Castlehill
The Royal Mile
Edinburgh EH1 2ND

UK £20.00
US $40.00

NATURE
www.luath.co.uk
ISBN 978-1-80425-241-3

9 781804 252413

54000

COVER IMAGES: REBECCA MARR
DESIGN: AMY TURNBULL